LONDON STREET PEOPLE
Past and Present

This book is for my Father and for my Mother

LONDON STREET PEOPLE
Past and Present

Bob Pullen

Lennard Publishing
1989

Lennard Publishing
a division of Lennard Books Ltd

Musterlin House
Jordan Hill Road
Oxford OX2 8DP

British Library Cataloguing in Publication Data
is available on this title.

ISBN: 1 85291 070 4

First published 1989
© Bob Pullen 1989

Phototypeset in Sabon by Jigsaw Graphics
Cover and book design by Pocknell & Co
Reproduced, printed and bound in Great Britain by
Butler & Tanner Ltd, Frome and London

CONTENTS

FOREWORD

London is much more than streets and buildings: it is a community of people. While London's varied architecture and the splendid vistas afforded by the Thames have exerted a strong pull on artists over the centuries, some painters and engravers have been equally fascinated by the city's inhabitants. One recalls the etchings of London street cries by Marcellus Lauron, published in 1687, and the charming late eighteenth-century paintings of street vendors by Francis Wheatley.

The early photographers were equally eager to record the people they encountered on their perambulations. Engravings after daguerrotypes by Richard Beard were published in Henry Mayhew's *London Labour and the London Poor* (1851), and in 1877 John Thomson issued some memorable photographs in a volume entitled *Street Life in London.*

It was Thomson's work which provided the impetus for Bob Pullen's project. In the photograph collection at Guildhall Library he later discovered two remarkable series of photographic postcards, both titled 'London Life' and published at the turn of the century by the Rotary Photographic Co. and J. Beagles Ltd. The idea of producing a comparative series of modern prints took root. Nowadays most Londoners appear to work in offices. Bob Pullen's photographs illustrate the varied economic activities that still take place in the open air. His then and now comparisons highlight the continuity of such occupations as roasting chestnuts and selling newspapers on street corners, and he draws our attention to more recent phenomena such as traffic wardens. (Will they still be part of the London scene in fifty years time?)

In creating this fascinating collection of photographs – archival copies of which can be seen at Guildhall Library – Bob Pullen has made an important contribution to London's social history. His prints gain in value from being placed in an historical context and will perhaps form the basis of a fresh then and now comparison a century hence.

John Fisher

*Deputy Keeper
of Prints and Maps,
Guildhall Library.*

INTRODUCTION

London's street people, traders and markets have long fascinated artists, writers, caricaturists, and photographers. Their history, along with the history of changing social and artistic attitudes to poverty, is encapsulated in the illustrated series of *Cries of London*, published from the seventeenth century onward. Early depictions of street traders were generalised picturesque types following Italian models, with little local character. A note of realism crept in with the immensely popular edition of *Cries* by Marcellus Lauron, (or Laroon) of 1687. This popularity was ironic in view of the attempts by the authorities of the day to limit severely the activities of hawkers, traders and beggars.

Indeed the story of London's street traders is full of repeated government attempts to control unruly traders, especially when they were selling seditious pamphlets and books. An alliance of sabbatarians, established merchants and tradesmen and the middle classes have always found common cause against the street people. Tudor London saw the passing of an act in Common Council forbidding costermongers to trade in the nave of Old St Paul's Cathedral, hitherto their chief place of business. During the reign of Elizabeth the Council attempted unsuccessfully to bar sellers from the lanes of the city so that they might be used as highways only. In the seventeenth century street traders were viewed as a lazy and unruly nuisance, and were accused of 'framing themselves a way whereby to live a more easy life than labour'.

From the fifteenth-century ballad *London Lyckpenny* onward, descriptions of the noise and confusion of London's streets, and particularly its disorientating effect on visiting countrymen, have been common in literature. Street vendors, with their strange and barbarous cries and dishevelled mien, have always been regarded as outsiders. Their depiction in art and literature before the nineteenth century always tended toward caricature – gin-sodden unipeds selling pies, or the picturesque – endless pictures of flower girls.

In the mid nineteenth century reforming writers, blurring the distinction between traders and beggars, saw the condition of the street people as emblematic of the state of the poor of London in general. Mayhew's monumental *London Labour and the London Poor*, first published in 1851, billed itself as 'the first attempt to publish the history of a people, from the lips of the people themselves'. Illustrated by Richard Beard's workmanlike portraits of street people, the book provides a vivid picture of a London hidden to most of Mayhew's readers. He makes no secret of his didactic intent, his hope being 'that the book may serve to give the rich a more intimate knowledge of the sufferings, and the frequent heroism under those sufferings, of the poor'.

Street Life in London, a monthly journal issued from February 1877 until January 1878 by the author and photographer John Thomson and the radical journalist Adolphe Smith, followed directly in this didactic reforming tradition. Many of the photographs in this volume are taken from it. Thomson saw the art of photography, still in its infancy, as having a primarily educative purpose as a means 'of expanding our knowledge of the world in which we live'. Whereas members of the public had taken to Thomson's depiction of street life in Hong Kong, they could not stomach the realism and apparent artlessness of the scenes of London, nor the quasi-scientific, ethnographic purpose of the series – which ran into financial trouble just after its launch. Following criticism from *Lloyds Weekly*, the series moved from the general to the specific with portraits of individuals such as *'Tickets' The Card Dealer* and the *London Boardman*.

Public reaction to the series was coloured by the sensational court case involving the use of fund-raising photographs by Dr Barnardo. Barnardo used a series of photos purporting to show the condition of waifs and orphans before and after they had been cared for by his charity. He was accused of falsely recreating their earlier condition. Though he was acquitted of any wrongdoing, the case shook public acceptance of the photograph as a documentary record.

In any case the technological limitations of early photography meant that each shot had to be carefully staged and the end result was often indistinguishable from the sentimental genre pieces or caricatures of contemporary prints and paintings. After the Barnardo case Thomson was at pains to avoid anything that smacked of artistic license. Political tensions between Smith, a long-standing member of the Social Democratic Federation, and Thomson further undermined the magazine, which folded in January of 1878.

Reforming interest in the situation of London's street people was partly due to their huge increase in numbers and visibility. Contemporary estimates, by Mayhew and others, of the numbers of people making their living wholly or partly from street vending in mid-nineteenth century London ranged from 30,000 to 100,000 adults. A range of social and economic factors were responsible for this sudden increase.

Firstly, the overall population of the metropolis had risen steeply from under one million at the turn of the century to two and a half million at the time of the Great Exhibition in 1851. Secondly, the expansion of the middle classes to new suburbs on the urban fringes displaced the poor into overcrowded inner city slums. Thirdly, the casual and piecemeal nature of inner city employment meant that there was a huge pool of casual unskilled labour tied to each locality. To compete with provincial factories manufacturers cut costs by having employees work in their own homes. Most enterprises had less than ten workers and could not afford to stockpile or to maintain production during lean times, leading to chronic unemployment and underemployment. Family members were often used as cheap labour, thus depressing wages further.

The unemployed thronged the streets seeking any means of making a living. Established traders such as costermongers, a feature of city life since the middle ages and the aristocracy of the street vendors, found themselves undermined by the new street people. Originally they were self-employed tradesmen selling a specialised line of their own produce such as fruit or game from the suburbs. Now they became middlemen in a chain of consumption and were vulnerable to price-fixing in a market which favoured established shop owners. They also faced fierce competition from newcomers for profitable pitches. For protection each district elected a costermongers 'king' to see off the occasionally violent intrusions by newcomers – particularly the Irish, who

had been arriving in large numbers since the 1830's. The position of 'Pearly King' often became hereditary and survives today.

Mayhew identified three groups of street traders – 'those who were bred to it, those who took to it out of love of a wandering life and those who were forced to it'. Of these groups, the largest by far was the last. Referred to by Engels as the 'surplus population', they took to street trading, hucksterism and crime. Seasonal work patterns added to the throng on the street. In winter brick layers took to hawking chestnuts, Irish dock labourers to selling fruit alongside their wives and children. Overabundance of traders, sub-standard goods, the yelling and obstruction from dawn to dusk as vendors were forced by falling margins to work longer hours, led to middle class outcry and repeated attempts by the metropolitan authorities to curb the noise and nuisance of the traders. However, draconian by-laws to limit their hours and haunts were often ineffectual, as necessity drove them to risk the penalty of the law.

Dickens gives us the flavour of a typical London morning in *Sketches by Boz*: 'Covent Garden market, and the avenues leading to it, are thronged with carts of all sorts, sizes and descriptions, from the heavy lumbering waggon, with its four stout horses, to the jiggling costermongers cart, with its comsumptive donkey. The pavement is already strewed with decayed cabbage leaves, broken hay-bands, and all the indescribable litters of a vegetable market; men are shouting, carts backing,

horses neighing, boys fighting, basket-women talking, piemen expatiating on the excellence of their pastry, and donkeys braying. These and a hundred other sounds form a compound discordant enough to a Londoner's ears, and remarkably disagreeable to those of country gentlemen who are sleeping at the Hummums for the first time.'

The sheer profusion of street trades described by Mayhew and Dickens gives us a picture of the vitality and hubbub of the Victorian streetscape: patterers, street doctors, spice sellers, crossing sweepers, beggars, rag-men, conjurers, balladeers, organ grinders with their monkeys, Ethiopian serenaders, boardmen, street-orderlies, cesspool sewermen, pure-finders, piemen, cats' meat dealers, water-cress sellers, Jewish clothesmen, mudlarks and flower-girls.

Whole tribes of Londoners lived on the rubbish and detritus of the metropolis. Pure-finders collected buckets of dog dung, used for purifying leather by the Bermondsey tanners. Bone-pickers and rag-gatherers trawled the streets for salvageable items of food and clothing to be sold wholesale for about sixpence a day. Cesspool-sewermen and 'toshers' worked below ground in the labyrnthine sewers on the river shore or cleaning the drains of houses. The work was dangerous – disease, disappearance in the maze and attack by rats were commonplace – but relatively profitable. Mayhew interviewed a cesspool-sewerman who was characteristically phlegmatic about the decline of his trade: "In time the

nightmen'll disappear; in course they must, there's so many new dodges comes up, always some one of the working classes is a being ruined. If it ain't steam, it's something else as knocks the bread out of their mouths quite as quick."

It was transience that impelled Smith and Thomson to photograph people in the nineteenth century, and it has also led me to undertake the modern photographs which complement their work in the pages which follow. I contrast the general street scenes of the past and the present, to show the former diversity of trades and activity on London's street: then I compare specific trades, past and present.

LONDON STREETS : PAST & PRESENT

COVENTRY STREET
[c. 1890]

Maul & Co

COVENTRY STREET
[today]

PICCADILLY
[c. 1890]

Maul & Co

PICCADILLY
[today]

OXFORD STREET
[c. 1890]

Photo anon

OXFORD STREET
[today]

NEAR SEVEN DIALS
[c. 1890]
Maul & Co

NEAR SEVEN DIALS
[today]

PICCADILLY CIRCUS
[c. 1890]

*Photo: George Washington
Wilson*

PICCADILLY CIRCUS
[today]

REGENT CIRCUS
[c. 1890]

*Photo: George Washington
Wilson*

OXFORD CIRCUS
[today]

ST. MARTIN'S LANE
[c. 1890]

Maul & Co

ST. MARTIN'S LANE
[today]

VANISHED STREET PEOPLE

STREET DOCTORS
[c. 1876]

Thomson/Smith

Despite the increasing number of free hospitals and access to professional medical care in Victorian London, street doctors, quacks and herbalists abounded. Evidently there was a great deal of resistance among the poor to the idea of charity relief. Visits to the hospital involved delays and bureaucracy, and many people preferred to treat themselves using the questionable remedies proffered by the street doctors. Travelling quacks were known as 'crocuses' because of the bogus Latin patter they used to sell their patent remedies. The itinerant medicine man in the photograph claimed to have taken up his calling after a miracle cure for his own failing eyesight.

PUBLIC DISINFECTORS
[c. 1876]
Thomson/Smith

The Metropolitan Board of Works was established in 1855 to tackle urban epidemics. As well as building 1,300 miles of sewers, it also appointed The Inspector of Public Nuisances and the Public Disinfectors. Infected persons were either removed to hospital, or confined to one room of their house until their recovery or demise. The Disinfectors, dressed in protective smocks and leggings, and pushing a hand-cart with their equipment, would then visit the house and remove the clothing, bedding, curtains and carpets, which was sent to the parish disinfecting oven. Contemporary theory held that disease was carried in dust, so the patient's room was disinfected by a laborious process involving spraying sulphur fumes, wallpaper stripping, dousing with acid and whitewashing.

MUSH-FAKERS
AND
GINGER-BEER MAKERS
[c. 1876]

Thomson/Smith

Ginger-beer was a popular summer drink in London. Selling it was an ideal opening for the unskilled urban poor. Ginger was boiled in a large container of water, then lemon, essence of cloves and sugar were added, together with yeast for effervesence. By the 1870's the street vendors had to compete with wholesale manufacturers. The best trade was to be found outside closed public houses on a Sunday morning, when thirsty, hungover drinkers would congregate to wait for opening time. Trade was seasonal and in the winter many of the Ginger-beer makers had to turn their hand to another trade. Mush-fakers provided a door to door service, collecting and mending umbrellas – 'mushrooms' – and also selling them in street markets like Petticoat Lane.

RECRUITING SERGEANTS
AT
WESTMINSTER
[c. 1876]
Thomson/Smith

The uncertain political situation of late nineteenth-century Europe meant that the Government had to maintain a large standing army at all times. Most recruiting was done around Westminster and Trafalgar Square and the photograph shows the sergeants outside the Mitre and Dove public house on King Street, a celebrated spot for enlisting. The sergeants, usually veterans from the Crimean war, received a guinea for each man enlisted. From their commission they had to pay each recruit an initial 'King's Shilling' as well as finding their uniforms and lodgings. Often the recruit would take the shilling and the drinks and then disappear, leaving the sergeant severely out of pocket. Still, some of them must have made a good living, as almost 3,000 men were enlisted at the Mitre and Dove in 1875.

FORTUNE TELLER
[c. 1918]

London Life Series
Rotary Photo

Fortune tellers, using birds in cages to foretell the future, were a common sight in the nineteenth century but probably something of a rarity by the time this photograph was taken. For a penny fee the bird would pick up little balls in response to questions about the future.

COVENT GARDEN PORTERS
[c. 1918]

London Life Series
Rotary Photo

The market at Covent Garden dates back to the seventeenth century, when the fifth Earl of Bedford was granted by royal charter the right to hold a market for flowers, fruit, roots and herbs, and to collect tolls from the traders.

In 1828, the makeshift stalls were cleared to make way for Charles Fowler's new market building.

The Covent Garden porters numbered almost one thousand in their heyday, and were supervised by twelve officials of the Bedford Estate and seven policemen hired from The Metropolitan Police. They seem to have favoured the round baskets of the type featured on the left of this photograph, perhaps because they could be stacked nine high.

The market was sold to the Covent Garden Market Authority in 1962 and in 1974 the market proper moved to Nine Elms, Vauxhall.

BIG BEN'S
TELESCOPE MAN
[c. 1910]

*London Life Series
Rotary Photo*

The Telescope Man, a well-known London character in the early part of the century, was photographed here in his customary spot beneath Queen Boudicca's statue on Westminster Bridge. For a small fee, tourists could see a close up of Big Ben's face. Besides this he sold maps, guides and sweets, and probably gave directions and advice to anybody needing them.

HAWKER
[c. 1918]

*London Life Series
Rotary Photo*

Walking the streets with his
wares arranged on a tray for
all to see, the street hawker
offered: shoe laces, pencils,
combs, matches, tooth picks,
ink pots and other small
everyday items for sale to the
busy passer-by. His function
has long since been overtaken
by the local newsagents' shop.

MATCH SELLER
[c. 1907]

Photo: F.G. Hodsoll

Many of the numerous
match sellers in London at
the turn of the century were
ex-servicemen. Retired or
disabled, and often without a
pension they were forced to
take to the streets selling
matches as a way of life only
marginally better than
beggary. The subject of
Hodsoll's photograph, to
judge by his bearing and
highly polished boots, was
almost certainly such an old
soldier down on his luck.

STREET PEOPLE : PAST & PRESENT

STREET ORDERLY MAN
[c. 1918]

*London Life Series
Rotary Photo*

We all pass by road sweepers, but we don't really notice them except when the pavement and wastebins are full of rubbish and we then wonder why we pay our rates. They will always be necessary because there will always be people and businesses which despoil our streets. London was without a comprehensive system of street-cleaning until

ROAD SWEEPER
BLOOMSBURY

the introduction of street
orderlies in 1834. The two
objectives at the time were to
provide employment for the
poor and a 'social and
salutiferous improvement to
street cleanliness'. The men in
both photographs have a
clean uniform which serves to
distance them from their
unsavoury task.

PAVIOURS, EAST END
OF
HOLBORN VIADUCT
[c. 1869]

Photo: Henry Dixon

In the City of London most road work is done at the weekends to minimise disruption to traffic. The paviours photographed in 1869 were working on one of the greatest building projects ever undertaken in the City. The Holborn Viaduct was designed by the City Surveyor, William Hayward, to bridge the valley of the Fleet, and to connect Holborn with Newgate Street. The Viaduct, some 1,400 feet long and 80 feet wide, was completed

ROAD MENDERS
CITY OF LONDON

after six years in 1869 at a
cost of two and a half million
pounds. Labouring gangs
were much larger in the
nineteenth century as much of
the material had to be
manhandled into place, and
the lack of heavy machinery
meant that work was slower
and more dangerous than
today. The gang in the
photograph were manually
ramming the road surface flat
with large, bollard-like
implements.

COVENT GARDEN FLOWER WOMEN
[c. 1876]

Thomson/Smith

The railings outside St. Paul's Church were a traditional pitch for flower girls. Covent Garden would have been a prime site for these 'girls' – often elderly married women ekeing out a precarious seasonal living. As Adolphe Smith wrote in 1876, a beat such as this 'is not merely the property of its present owners, it has been inherited from previous generations of flower women'. Less fortunate traders were forced by police by-laws to stand in the roadway selling posies with their traditionally plaintiff cries of, 'Won't you buy my sweet lavender' and, 'Buy my pretty flowers'.

FLOWER GIRL
COVENT GARDEN

Flower girls usually wore a distinctive costume of shawls and befeathered hats, selling their posies and buttonholes from baskets or 'shallows'. The costume and the cry are mimicked by their modern successors catering for the nostalgia market in the tourist bazaar of Covent Garden. Nowadays the job is not taken from sheer necessity and passed from mother to daughter, but more likely a stop-gap on the way to something else – "I've been working at this part-time since April. There are about five of us but my profession is singing."

STREET ADVERTISING
[c. 1876]

Thomson/Smith

The poster being pasted up in
the earlier photograph
announces a new waxwork at
Madame Tussauds, of
William Fish, the Blackburn
murderer. At the time of the
photograph there were
around 200 men employed
full time by various
contractors to paste bills
around London. For the
contractors it was a lucrative
business, and up to £60,000
was paid each year for the hire
of hoardings and wall space
in the capital. Just as today
the notice 'Bill Stickers Will

BILL STICKER
COVENT GARDEN

Be Prosecuted' does little to discourage the hordes of determined pasters, so in Victorian London the work of the regulars was supplemented by squads of fly-pasters. They were often sent out to cover every available wall space on the routes to important events such as the Boat Race. Fierce competition between contractors meant that posters were often over-pasted and the teams of fly-pasters would have to be sent out two or three times a day.

HALF-PENNY ICES
[c. 1876]

Thomson/Smith

"I work only at the weekends. In the week I have a full-time job in an office. I start about 10 a.m. and work through until 4 p.m. It gets dark then and there aren't many people about. When the sun comes out everyone wants an ice-cream."

Ice cream has been a cheap and popular street refreshment since the beginning of the nineteenth century. Italian ice cream sellers were a familiar sight throughout London. Their chief haunts were Clerkenwell, Saffron Hill and Hatton Garden, possibly because of their large Italian populations. In common with

ICE-CREAM SELLER
SERPENTINE

other street traders they were regularly accused of spreading disease through lack of hygiene, leading to the taunt that the ice-cream seller's patter went, 'What'll you 'ave, Straby, Vaniller or Microbe'. Vendors made their own ice-cream and pushed their barrow to the pitch, and then as now, the prime sites were near a park, fair or public entertainment where they could be sure of good passing trade from thirsty promenaders. Customers were often attracted by means of a song or bell and the electronic chimes of today's ice-cream vans follow that tradition.

FLYING DUSTMEN
[c. 1876]

Thomson/Smith

"On Saturdays we start work about 6.30 a.m. and go on until 9 a.m. – we give a good collection, the City is clean." Present-day dustmen are usually employed by the local council, and their constant service, swallowing the proliferation of rubbish spawned by the twentieth century, is taken for granted. In the nineteenth century, the collection of refuse was a speculative and lucrative business operated by a number of wealthy contractors paid by the parish authorities. They owned the horses, carts and baskets used by dustmen who were hired on a daily basis. They also controlled the dustyards where the sorting of dust was

DUSTBIN MEN
CITY OF LONDON

an industry in itself, with hundreds of men and women employed to sieve dust which was either sold as manure or to brickmakers.

The 'flying dustmen' in the photograph were freelance collectors who made their illegal rounds hoping to pick up saleable items. With their cry of 'Dust o' they would try to attract the attention of householders while avoiding the Inspector of Public Nuisances. All dustmen at this time worked in pairs, the 'filler' emptying the dustbins into his baskets while the 'carrier' would mount the ladder on the side of the boxcart and deposit the refuse inside.

THE OLD CLOTHES
OF
ST GILES
[c. 1876]

Thomson / Smith

In the nineteenth century, second-hand clothes were often touted by itinerant street vendors. Jewish traders also sold at thriving markets in Petticoat Lane and especially Houndsditch. Monmouth Street, off Seven Dials in Covent Garden, was particularly noted for its second-hand clothes shops which were described by Dickens in *Sketches by Boz*. The poor relied on the 'hand-me-downs' of the middle classes as offered at the St Giles stall. Ready made clothing was still rare and made-to-measure items were too expensive. During a visit to London in the late 1860's, Hippolyte Taine professed

SECOND-HAND
CLOTHES SELLER
COVENT GARDEN

himself shocked at the readiness of the urban poor to don the tawdry cast-offs of the rich, in contrast to the simple working clothes of the French artisan and peasant classes. Covent Garden is still a centre for second-hand clothes shops and stalls, mostly catering for specialised period styles sought by the young and fashionable rather than by the needy. "I work here for three days out of the week. I've been setting up here for the last few months. I have a licence, it doesn't cost much and I do O.K. here. When it rains I have a cover so the clothes don't get wet!"

A CITY
WINDOW CLEANER
[c. 1918]

*London Life Series
Rotary Photo*

The basic equipment of the
window cleaner has changed
little in the interval between
the two photographs. The
convex triangular ladder, the
bucket and the cleaning mops
and rags have still to be
heaved about from job to job,
whatever the weather.
The cleaner in the old

WINDOW CLEANER
SPITALFIELDS

photograph cannot have
faced the problems of
cleaning huge plate glass
windows from a swaying
suspended platform, many
storeys above the pavement,
but the job has always been
one which entailed a deal of
agility and a good head for
heights.

THE BREWER'S MAN
[c. 1918]

London Life Series
Rotary Photo

The drayman's job has hardly changed in the years separating the two photographs. Barrels are unloaded from a platform onto sacking on the pavement, then lowered into the cellar of the public house using a rope. In 1918 the beer would have been transported using a dray pulled by two shire horses. Lorries are more

DRAYMAN
BLOOMSBURY

common now, but some
breweries, such as Whitbread
& Co in Chiswell Street,
continue the practice of
keeping shire horses to deliver
their beer to a few clients
within the City of London.
Barrels are now made of
aluminium instead of oak
and the switch to metal made
thousands of coopers
redundant.

A WOMAN PAVEMENT
ARTIST
[c. 1918]

London Life Series
Rotary Photo

"I started here today. I hope I
won't be moved on. I was at
Tower Bridge but the police
moved me on. I've been doing
this for four years. I am
hoping to get a job painting
murals."
In many busy places around
London you see the work of
these pavement artists – most
of their work is copied from

PAVEMENT ARTIST
CROYDON

plates or postcards of
famous paintings, portraits,
landscapes or religious
scenes. The life of a pavement
artist cannot have altered
much since 1918. Working
in chalk they receive 'tributes'
to their skill while the work
is in progress – perhaps an
early form of performance art!

THE POSTMAN
[c. 1918]

London Life Series
Beagles Postcards

"I've been a postman most of my life, but in a few months time I will be retiring."
The postman's day, with its early start, long daily round of walking, and day to day contact with the public whom he serves, cannot be greatly different from that of his Victorian predecessor. The modern postman may have to carry his load of post about the streets, but he does not face the awesome task of up to fifteen separate deliveries per day. This was commonplace in London up to the early part of this century, with letters being charged at the standard rate of one penny.
The Penny Post of the nineteenth century offered a cheap, popular and efficient method of communication within London. Several hundred receiving houses forwarded the pre-paid letters to seven main sorting houses from which more than ten

POSTMAN
MAYFAIR

deliveries a day went out.
However, the system was
open to corruption.
Receiving houses were known
to destroy the correspondence
and pocket the one penny
postage fee. For a time the
system was changed to allow
post to be sent unpaid, with
the increased charge of two
pence levied at the receiving
end. This led to further
problems with many
addressees finding themselves
unable to find the postage fee,
so that the letter had to be
returned to the sender. Finally
in the 1840's the Penny Post
was re-established. Letters
were charged by weight and
postage was paid by the
sender using the world's
first adhesive stamp, the
Penny Black.
Letters continued to be
charged at the same rate until
about the time of this
photograph, when the Penny
Post became the Penny
Ha'penny Post.

'TICKETS'
THE CARD-DEALER
[c. 1876]

Thomson/Smith

"I paint vans, shop fronts, anything really. I just took it up one day. No-one trained me. I've been doing this for thirty years."

The profession of sign-writing has been in steady decline in the interval between the two photographs. The disappearance of wooden shop-fascias and the easy availability of cheap mechanical methods of typesetting signs mean that the hand-painted shop sign is now something of a rarity. 'Tickets', a French immigrant to London by way of Canada and America, had a chequered career in many menial positions, detailed by Thomson and Smith, before ending up as a seller of tickets – hand-painted cards and advertisements placed in shop

SIGN WRITER
CLERKENWELL

windows. Working with a
partner who did most of the
painting, 'Tickets' would
wander the streets looking for
shops with old and
discoloured cards, then try to
persuade the owner of the
need for new, more elaborate,
tickets. From this trade he
could only make a poor living
of between four and fifteen
shillings a week after costs.
His plight came to the
attention of George Moore, a
well known merchant and
philanthropist of the time,
who advanced him money for
premises and materials.
'Tickets' hoped that the new
success of the business would
allow him to return to France
as a shopkeeper, but it is not
known if this simple ambition
was realised.

DISTRICT MESSENGER
BOY
[c. 1918]

London Life Series
Rotary Photo

"I started last September and
will finish this September, in
time for college. I'm self-
employed so when I've had
enough for the day I go home.
Luckily I've just picked up
two parcels for the same place
so I get paid twice."
Courier and messenger
services have grown hugely
over the last few years. In the
past the Post Office provided
many of the services which

BICYCLE MESSENGER
HOXTON

are now the exclusive preserve
of private companies. The
District Messengers would
have delivered urgent letters,
parcels and telegrams. Now
the Post Office has little use
for bicycles and the uniformed
boys have been replaced by
hundreds of young people on
mountain bikes, distinctively
dressed in brightly coloured
cycling costumes.

NEWSPAPER BOY
[c. 1918]

London Life Series
Rotary Photo

"I've been doing this for
about one and a half years. In
school time I start about 6
o'clock, but in holiday time a
little later. It's quicker by bike
– thirty to forty minutes – on
foot it takes about an hour."
The paper boy now is most
likely a schoolboy
supplementing his pocket
money with an early morning
round on his bicycle. For the

NEWSPAPER BOY
FOREST HILL

paper boy of 1918 it was a
full-time job, perhaps for life.
Instead of one edition per day
he would sell the extras and
special editions which, before
radio and television, were the
only source of daily news
available. Working
throughout the day in all
weathers, his constant refrain
was, 'papers for sale – read
the latest news'.

GLAZIER
'MEND YER WINDOWS'
[c. 1884]
*Charles Spurgeon Greenwich
Local History Library,
Greenwich*

"This is my first job. I've been working for this company for four years. I'm putting double-glazing in this block of flats."

We can see that in 1884 the glazier carried the glass around on his back, which

GLAZIER
LOWER SYDENHAM

must have been quite
heavy. Walking the streets
with his cry of, 'mend
yer windows', his line of
work depended to an
unusual extent on being
in the right place at the
right time.

THE BUTCHER'S BOY
[c. 1918]

*London Life Series
Beagles Postcards*

Butchers are one of the few traders who still deliver their wares directly to the customer. Up to the middle part of this century it was commonplace for almost all domestic consumables to be delivered to those who could afford it.

The smartly turned-out butcher boy in the earlier photo carries the cuts of meat on a wooden platter on his shoulder. The wood would

BUTCHER'S BOY
CITY OF LONDON

then be scrubbed down at the
end of each day. Speed of
delivery was vital as
households and most
butchers would not have had
cold storage. Bicycles were not
commonly used for deliveries
until the 1890's. Less
sartorially elegant but
speedier, the modern
butcher's boy bikes the
shrink-wrapped meat direct
from the cold store to the
customer's kitchen.

THE LONDON BOARDMAN
[c. 1876]

Thomson/Smith

"I've been doing this for a few weeks, advertising the new market at St Martin-in-the-Fields. I usually start about 11.30 a.m. and go on to 4 p.m.. Come Easter I will dress up as an Easter bunny." Unlike their Victorian counterparts, modern boardmen can walk on the pavements. In the nineteenth century it could be a hazardous occupation. Boardmen were compelled to walk on the streets amid the bustle of carriages, cabs and omnibuses. They frequently

BOARDMAN
OXFORD STREET

suffered abuse from teasing
children throwing mud at
their boards, and they had no
protection from bad weather.
According to Thomson and
Smith, the boardmen came
from all walks of life and
represented all those 'who
have gone to the wall . . . some
are hopelessly vulgar and
ignorant, others have received
the education of a gentleman.'
The boardman in the old
photograph is advertising
'Renovo', a patent cleaner
for fabrics.

ITALIAN STREET
MUSICIANS
[c. 1876]

Thomson/Smith

London has a long tradition of street musicians, from the medieval troubadours and minstrels to the popular street ballad singers of the seventeenth and eighteenth centuries. In the mid-nineteenth century Mayhew recorded more than 250 ballad singers in London and many more street instrumentalists. Their ranks were swelled by an influx of Italian immigrants who introduced mechanical organs and harps. Street musicians, as today, were often seen as little more than

MUSICIAN
SOUTH BANK

a nuisance. In 1864 a Police
Act was introduced which
allowed complaints to the
police who would then move
the musicians on. Many
writers, including Dickens
and Tennyson, supported the
Act, on the grounds that
passing street musicians
disturbed their work. Buskers
today face the same problems
and are liable to be moved on
from their pitches in
underground stations and
shopping precincts. The
South Bank is one of the few
sites where busking is
officially tolerated.

THE SELLER OF
SHELL FISH
[c. 1876]

Thomson/Smith

"I'm 78 years old. I've been doing this for 48 years. I started up myself but I do have a friend who helps. I only work Sundays. I was up at 5 a.m. at the market and I work until 12.30 p.m. I've been on television- Timewatch, Minder, and Candid Camera. In Candid Camera I pretended to swallow a gold fish but really it was a piece of carrot."

Thomson and Smith recorded the advice given by the shellfish seller of 1876 as being to 'find out a prime thirsty spot, which you know

SHELLFISH SELLER
KENSAL TOWN

by the number of public
'ouses it supports'. As can
be seen from the Kensal Town
photograph this advice still
holds good, as the trader
stands poised to benefit from
the passing business of those
eager for an appetizer on their
way to the pub. Both men
probably bought their wares
at the same market –
Billingsgate. A major
difference is the menu on
offer. In 1876, oysters were a
staple of the poor and sold
cheaply by the pint from
thousands of stalls in the
poorer parts of the city.

CLAPHAM COMMON INDUSTRIES 'WAITING FOR HIRE'
[c. 1876]

Thomson / Smith

"I've been here forty years. I took over from my father and he took over from his father. The track was specially laid for him. But my girl is not interested in the donkey ride, so I don't know what will happen."

Most places of public recreation had donkey rides at one time but they are now rare. In 1877 there were two firms offering rides on Clapham Common, the

Donkey Ride
Blackheath Common

largest having twenty to twenty-five donkeys. The donkeys were generally bought at the start of the season, the female being preferred, as they were said to give a smoother ride, and could be sold at a premium when in foal at the end of the season. Then, as now, the donkey keeper was busiest on public holidays and depended on his children to help with the work.

CITY POLICE
CONSTABLE
[c. 1910]

*London Life Series
Rotary Photo*

"I have been a special
constable for a few years now.
We train for about 20 weeks –
one night a week. Of course
we don't know as much as the
Metropolitan Police but we
come in useful especially at
events like this (Chinese New
Year). I feel as though I am
putting something back into
the community."
The Metropolitan Police force
was formed by Robert Peel in
1829 amidst great public
hostility and suspicion. The
force replaced the inadequate
system of watchmen which
had existed in one form or
another since the Statute of
Westminster of 1285. Peel's
major political opposition to
the reforms came from the
City. He therefore agreed to
exclude the City from the
scope of his police bill in
return for their tacit support.

SPECIAL CONSTABLE
OFF LEICESTER SQUARE

For ten years the City maintained its archaic City Day Police force. The 1839 City of London Police Act marked a complete re-organisation of the force under the command of a commissioner and the overall authority of the City Corporation. By 1910, when this photograph was taken, the force had reached it's maximum strength of some 1,181 men. Until 1946 City of London Police had no jurisdiction outside the Square Mile. The Special Constabulary has been diminishing in size and importance since World War Two. It consists in the main of unpaid, part-time volunteers, who undertake specific policing tasks such as traffic control and patrolling a beat.

THE COSTERMONGER
[c. 1918]

London Life Series
Beagles Postcards

"I set up about 10.30 a.m. – it takes a while but it's got to look good – this helps to sell the fruit. I could put one person here and he would take £30 a day – I could put someone else here and they could take £300, the difference is presentation. I've been working stalls since before I was 16."
Costermongers got their name from the costard, a type of large ribbed apple. In the nineteenth century the name was generally applied to traders selling fish, fruit and vegetables from a fixed stall in a street market or, as in the photograph, walking the streets with a barrow or basket. Then, a successful costermonger made a relatively good living, often earning more than a skilled artisan. Unemployment and Irish immigration in the mid-nineteenth century swelled their ranks.
Mayhew estimated that there

COSTERMONGER
CHARING CROSS ROAD

were at least 30,000 traders on the streets in 1851. Competition for profitable pitches was fierce. To protect themselves the established costermongers banded together with each district under the leadership of a Pearly King – probably the largest and most aggressive among them. These Pearly Kings & Queens decorated their clothes with numerous mother-of-pearl buttons, often spelling out the district of their 'reign'. Their positions often became hereditary and survive today in a more picturesque form. As today, presentation was very important, but because their wares were not of first quality, and because of a general suspicion that contaminated fruit caused epidemics, the costermongers generally sold only to the poor who could not afford to go to shops.

HOT CHESTNUT SELLER
[c. 1918]

London Life Series
Rotary Photo

"It's a nice day today. I work the seasons, hot chestnuts now and ice creams in the summer. I usually work from half-past ten until there are no people about. I've been arrested three times for obstructing the highway, but I don't get in people's way. An American asked how much the brazier costs – it's about £300."
Despite the fact that over eighty years separates the two photographs, there is no

HOT CHESTNUT SELLER
CHARING CROSS ROAD

appreciable difference. Both men use a similar type of barrow and brazier. Both do their best trade on cold autumn and winter days, when the chestnuts are in season and when passers-by like to keep their hands and stomachs warm, cheered by the warmth of the roaring brazier. The seller of 1918 wears his trading license on his arm; his successor risks repeated fines for obstructing the highway.

LIFE GUARD
WHITEHALL
[c. 1890]

Photo: F.G.O.S

The Life Guard's duty has
remained essentially
unchanged. Between 10 a.m.
and 4 p.m. throughout the
week they are on guard, two
on horseback and two
dismounted. Their duty is not
continuous as they are
regularly relieved by other
members of the troop.
There are two regiments who
mount sentry at the Horse
Guards: the Life Guards and
the Royal Horse Guards, both

LIFE GUARD
WHITEHALL

dating back to the
seventeenth century. At
11 a.m. daily (and 10 a.m.
on Sundays) the Changing
of the Guards takes place.
This ceremony attracts
many tourists who come
to take photographs, not
just of the main event, but
also of their friends who
stand beside the mounted
sentry, hoping that the
horse does not take a nip out
of them!

TOLL GATE KEEPER
KENSINGTON
OLD TOLL GATE
[c. 1890]

"I've been doing this ten years this November. I work from 7.30 a.m. to 2 p.m., two days on and one day off. Then the next shift is from 2.30 p.m. to 8.30 p.m."

Until the mid nineteenth century there were numerous toll gates in London. The toll gate at Kensington, which was abolished in 1864, gave passage from Kensington to Knightsbridge. Then, as now, the tariffs charged varied according to the type of vehicle; wheels of 6″ width would pay one toll and 9″ width a lesser toll, as the 6″ wheels would cause greater

TOLL GATE KEEPER
DULWICH

damage to the road. The money collected was used to maintain the roads. London's last remaining toll gate was set up in 1789 by John Morgan to pay for his private road, leading to grazing land leased from the College of God's Gift at Dulwich. The toll gate was taken over by the college in 1809 and continues to pay for the road's maintenance. The current rates are ten pence for cars and fifty pence for lorries. The idea of using a toll system to cover the costs of new roads has recently been revived.

LINEMAN, HOLBORN
[c. 1900]

British Telecom

"I've been with them for nine years. I deal with everything outside. In winter they give you warm clothing." Although the majority of cables are now underground, the lineman in 1900, an employee of the National Telephone Company, would have worked high above the roofs of London. Most of the local authorities insisted that

TELECOM ENGINEER
HOXTON

cables be hoisted high to avoid
interference with sewers and
tube lines. The erecting and
maintenance of lines was
hard and dangerous work.
Linemen would often walk up
to twenty-five miles a day,
telescope in hand, to spot
faults. Despite the long hours
and high winds the lineman's
motto was 'faults must be
cleared at all hazards'.

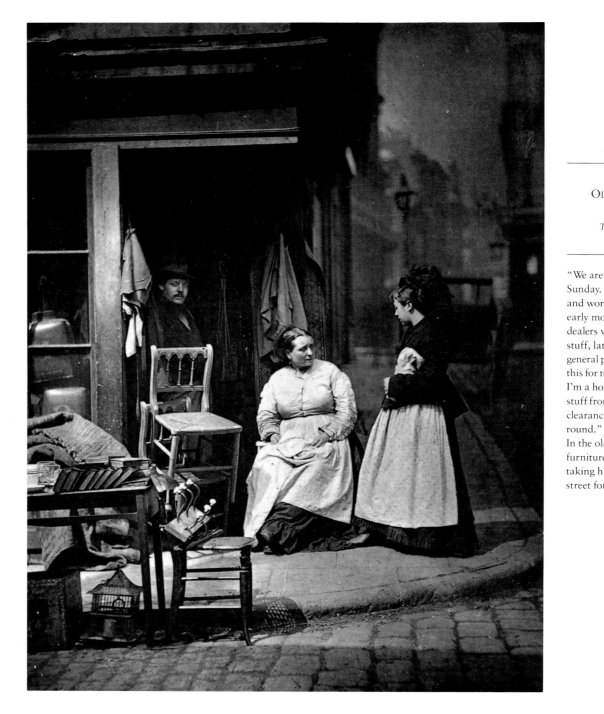

OLD FURNITURE
[c. 1876]

Thomson/Smith

"We are only here on a
Sunday. I start about 8 a.m.
and work until 2 p.m. In the
early morning we get the
dealers who buy up the good
stuff, later on we get the
general public. I've been doing
this for ten years – in the week
I'm a housewife. We get our
stuff from auctions and house
clearances. We work all year
round."
In the old photograph the
furniture dealer can be seen
taking his stock onto the
street for display. According

OLD FURNITURE DEALER
OFF BRICK LANE

to Adolphe Smith, 'furniture dealers of this class, that is to say, the men who cater for the poor, generally obtain their stock from brokers and bailiffs' and 'buy up the entire furniture of a poor household for a given sum'. Evidently the second-hand furniture business has changed little in the intervening years except that today hunting for good second-hand furniture in unlikely places is not confined to the poor.

LONDON CABMAN
[c. 1876]

Thomson/Smith

"I work about 5 days a week. I don't work nights although it's good pay. I've been a taxi-driver for the past 38 years. It's a good job, the time is my own. You have to have patience waiting for a fare." The history of London's various cab services has been characterised by repeated legislation to protect the customer from overcharging and risk to life and limb. By the late eighteenth century the Hackney coach system was in disarray. Many carriages were filthy and unsafe, drivers demanded huge tips and often raced each other in the streets and licenses were doled out in return for bribes and favours. The 1832 Stage Carriages Act and the introduction of new two-seater cab designs, such as the Hansom cab seen in the photograph, improved safety and comfort. By 1904 there were

TAXI DRIVER
CITY OF WESTMINSTER

7,499 two-wheel hansoms and 3,905 4-wheel 'growlers'. Victorian cabmen had a reputation for heavy-drinking, leading several philanthropists to establish a number of 'Cabmen's Shelters' where drivers could have cheap meals and hot, non-alcoholic drinks. Smith recorded in 1876 that cabmen 'despite their rough appearance and quarrelsome tone [were] as a rule reliable and honest men'. Petrol engined cabs, licensed by the Metropolitan Police, were introduced in 1904, and further regulated by the introduction of the Taximeter in 1907. This gave the cabs their new name and put an end to disputes over fares. Metal flags, which were pulled down when the taxi was hired, survived until 1959, when the present illuminated 'for hire' signs were introduced.

GEORGE WOLLARD
GARDENER AT ST. PAUL'S
[c. 1912]

Photo anon

"I've been in the job twenty years. I usually work in one specific area. Winter or summer the hours are 7.30 a.m. to 4.30 p.m. but of course in winter I work a lot less due to the cold and lack of light. We provide all the flowers for the offices and parks in Lewisham. In the

STREET
STREET
PEOPLE
PAST
AND
PRESENT

97

GARDENER
CATFORD

offices the flowers can only
stay a few weeks – then they
have to go into the greenhouses
to recover."
George Wollard, the gardener
of St. Paul's must, like all
gardeners, have been proud of
the garden he tended. His
garden would have given
pleasure to all who visited the
cathedral.

THE MILKMAN
[c. 1910]

London Life Series
Rotary Photo

"I've been a milkman for 8 years. I changed companies a couple of months ago, but I'm still doing the same work. Before this I worked in an office so it was a bit of a change. I like to work in the open."

In the late nineteenth century, many dairies still kept their cows in the centre of London. Because of the risk of disease the government moved to regulate the often unhygienic conditions of cowhouses and dairies with the Contagious Diseases (Animals) Act of 1879. Thereafter dairies were supplied chiefly from farms on the borders of London with large herds in the meadows of Islington,

MILKMAN
FOREST HILL

Camden Town and Battersea Fields. Improved railway connections allowed dairies to have contracts with farms even further afield. As can be seen from the plaque on the front of the hand-cart, milk from special breeds such as the 'Alderney' were kept for infants and invalids. In much the same way as today, the milkman had a daily round of regular customers; milk was delivered originally using 10 gallon drums borne on a yoke across the milkman's shoulders. Later a three-wheel hand-cart, such as that seen in the photograph, was used with the milk being delivered in small cans.

CLAPHAM COMMON
INDUSTRIES
'PHOTOGRAPHY
ON THE COMMON'
[c. 1876]

Thomson/Smith

Clapham Common was not
only a place of public
recreation but also provided a
living for the many vendors,
entertainers and caterers.
Among them were several
photographers who
frequented the Common
during the season from
March to Whitsuntide. Their
best customers were children's
nannies who, having
presented one photograph of
their charges to their
mistresses, were invariably
'commissioned to obtain one
or more likenesses on [their]
next visit to the Common'.
"I work mainly on my spare
days. I don't do this all day, as
I have a full-time job. Usually
I go to an area and walk
around looking for people to
photograph. Central London

PHOTOGRAPHER
FOREST HILL

is a good place to wander
about, but sometimes on my
way out or returning home I
have come across people to
photograph. In the early days
of my project I took many
photographs of the most
obvious jobs, but as it
progressed, it became
difficult to find anyone to
photograph, so it became a
day of walking the camera.
There are still street traders
that I have yet to photograph,
such as a 'shoe shine boy',
although I know where there
is supposed to be one and
have visited his haunt many
times, I have yet to find him.
Luck has played a large part
in obtaining some of my
photographs, but for this last
photograph, none was
involved!".

TODAY'S STREET PEOPLE

PUNCH AND JUDY MAN
COVENT GARDEN

"I've been working here since
the craft market opened
about eight years ago. My
father Percy Press the First
was also a Punch and Judy
man. I travel all over the
world."
The Punch and Judy show has
been a part of London street
entertainment, particularly in
Covent Garden, since the
seventeenth century when it
first arrived from Italy.

BOOKSELLER
COVENT GARDEN

In this street there are many different stalls selling anything from books to vegetables, shellfish to second-hand clothes. The second-hand bookseller's trade depends on the occassional passer-by, stopping to browse among his books. He has to dress for cold and wet weather and protect his books from the rain, unlike the booksellers around the corner in Charing Cross Road.

"We work a shift system, but we do a two and a half day week. We give out information to tourists, usually about how to get to places of interest. We are funded by the Manpower Services Commission. You're doing one job for up to a year."

BALLOON SELLER
TRAFALGAR SQUARE

"I've only been in the job a
week. I don't just work here
but also at Madame
Tussauds. I usually start at
11 a.m. and finish around
6 p.m. If it rains we don't
work but still get paid."

TRAFFIC WARDENS
CITY OF LONDON

In central London we tend to
notice the traffic wardens as
they walk around their daily
beat, issuing parking tickets,
checking meters and generally
helping the police to prevent
traffic congestion. A traffic
warden receives three weeks
training in the 'classroom'
and then two weeks outside
with a 'parent warden'
before he or she is allowed to
work alone.

METER MECHANIC
CITY OF LONDON

"I've been in the job about three months, before this I was an electrician. This job is okay, you're your own boss. There are about thirty of us in London and one hundred and fifty in the country."

RESCUE ARCHAEOLOGIST
CITY OF LONDON

The archaeologist is charting
what there is on the ground
below him in the face of the
threat of redevelopment. On
this site, in the Guildhall
Courtyard, the remains of
London's Roman
Amphitheatre have been
found. The proposed building
of the Guildhall Art Gallery
has been delayed while the dig
is in progress.

MARKET RESEARCHER
CATFORD

"I work part-time for Gallup.
Today I am interviewing
women about cooking. I
cover the Blackheath/Catford
area. I work part-time which
suits me as my husband is the
new MP in Glasgow."

R.A.C. SERVICE
PATROL MAN
COVENT GARDEN

"I've been in the motor
industry for eight years and
with this for three. It's a nice
job – there's lots of freedom."

LOLLIPOP MAN
FOREST HILL

"I've been doing this for the
past eight years – another two
years to go until I am seventy-
five years old then that will be
it. I used to work nights –
twenty-five years as a printer
– but I like working out
of doors."

CARRIAGE
MAINTENANCE MEN
HYDE PARK

The marking of the roads is
an essential service designed
to keep motorists, cyclists and
pedestrians in their respective
lanes. In Hyde Park most of
the roads are divided between
cyclists and pedestrians, so on
a sunny day we can walk
around the park without
being run over.

COOKERMAN
CAMDEN

"I've been doing this since
1948."

SITE INVESTIGATORS
COVENT GARDEN

"We bore down thirty metres,
taking samples every metre,
to see what the ground is like.
We go all over the country, but
mainly in the south-east."

ROOFERS
CATFORD

Man on left – "I've been
working at this ten years, it's
my own firm. It's hard work –
only last week the other bloke
got sun-stroke." Man on
right – "I've been working for
three months. It's hard work.
It takes about a week to put a
roof on."

118   LONDON
       STREET
       PEOPLE

WELDER
COVENT GARDEN

This welder has a busy day erecting swings and ensuring that they are safe for small children to play on in the park behind St Giles-in-the-Fields Church, in the centre of London.

SANDWICH DELIVERY
BOY
CITY OF LONDON

In the morning the office
workers in the City phone in
their orders for lunch. After
11.30 the delivery boy goes
out on his bike, weighed
down with sandwiches and
rolls to provide a quick lunch
to desk-bound brokers and
market makers.

PAINTERS
SOHO

This photograph was taken over a year ago when two painters were whitewashing the side of the building. Since then a colourful mural has been painted.

BICYCLE ADVERTISER
COVENT GARDEN

"I've been doing this for
about two weeks. A friend at
Westminster Council phoned
me about cycling around. I
work from 10 a.m. to 6 p.m."

STONE MASON
TRAFALGAR SQUARE

"We clean the column and the
fountains. We do this every
few years. My friend was
photographed with Nelson a
few weeks ago and was in
the paper."

CRISTOF THE CLOWN
COVENT GARDEN

"I have a certain time here.
When I start I try to get the
kids to stop and take part,
once that happens a crowd
gathers. I come from
Australia. I've worked all over
the world. Soon I will be
going to Japan.
Street performance is very
popular there!"

NEWSPAPER SELLER
CHARING CROSS

This newspaper seller only works at the weekends, selling papers to a core of regular customers and to passing strangers. During the week it's the hard political and financial news of the day but on Sundays the typical English pursuits of scandalmongering, murder and gardening hold sway.

RELIEF MARKET
INSPECTOR
BRICK LANE

"I check the stalls. Some are
licensed, some not. I see that
the commodities that are on
the stalls are what they are
supposed to sell. I collect the
pink slips which they buy so I
don't collect any money. I do
this at the week-end, during
the week I'm in the office."

DOORMAN
FORTNUM & MASONS
PICCADILLY

"I've been a doorman nearly all my life. I've been here nine years. I start at 9 a.m. and finish at 5 p.m., five days a week."

ACKNOWLEDGEMENTS

Firstly I would like to give thanks to the Guildhall Library who provided the funding for the original project.

My thanks to Ralph Hyde, Keeper of Prints and Maps for his support;
to John Fisher his Deputy for his comments,
and Jeremy Smith who will always have my special gratitude;
and finally to Shirley Leverell for her typing.

I would especially like to thank Hilary Callan for her considerable help, particularly with the Introduction.

OLD PHOTOGRAPHS

The photographs listed below are from the London Life Postcard series, published either by Rotary Photo (R.P.) or Beagles Postcards (B.P.).

82	The Costermonger	c. 1918	B.P.
60	The Postman	c. 1918	B.P.
70	The Butcher's Boy	c. 1918	B.P.
35	Covent Garden Porters	c. 1918	R.P.
84	Hot Chestnut Seller	c. 1918	R.P.
64	District Messenger Boy	c. 1918	R.P.
58	A Woman Pavement Artist	c. 1918	R.P.
37	Hawker	c. 1918	R.P.
66	Newspaper Boy	c. 1918	R.P.
56	The Brewer's Man	c. 1918	R.P.
40	Street Orderly Man	c. 1918	R.P.
54	A City Window Cleaner	c. 1918	R.P.
34	Fortune Teller	c. 1918	R.P.
36	Big Ben's Telescope Man	c. 1910	R.P.
80	City Police Constable	c. 1910	R.P.
98	The Milkman	c. 1910	R.P.
96	George Wollard, Gardener of St. Pauls	c. 1912	*anon.*
38	Match Seller	c. 1907	*By F. G. Hodsoll*
68	Glazier 'Mend Yer Windows'	c. 1884	*By Charles Spurgeon, courtesy of Greenwich Local History Library, Greenwich.*
42	Paviours, East end of Holborn Viaduct	c. 1869	*By Henry Dixon*
86	Life Guard, Whitehall	c. 1890	*By FGOS*

PRESENT DAY PHOTOGRAPHS

The photographs listed below are from *Street Life in London* written by Adolphe Smith, with photography by John Thomson.

78	Clapham Common Industries 'Waiting for a Hire'	c. 1876
44	Covent Garden Flower Women	c. 1876
50	Flying Dustmen	c. 1876
48	Half Penny Ices	c. 1876
74	Italian Street Musicians	c. 1876
94	London Cabman	c. 1876
32	Mush-Fakers and Ginger Beer Makers	c. 1876
31	Public Disinfecters	c. 1876
33	Recruiting Sergeants at Westminster	c. 1876
46	Street Advertising	c. 1876
30	Street Doctors	c. 1876
72	The London Boardman	c. 1876
52	The Old Clothes of St. Giles	c. 1876
76	The Seller of Shell Fish	c. 1876
62	'Tickets', The Card-dealer	c. 1876
92	Old Furniture	c. 1876
100	Clapham Common Industries 'Photography on the Common'	c. 1876

The photograph of an overhead lineman (page 90) is reproduced courtesy of British Telecommunications, that of a toll keeper (page 88) courtesy of The Museum of London.

I would like to give thanks to the Guildhall Library who provided all other photographs.